AF489704

Eyes Wide

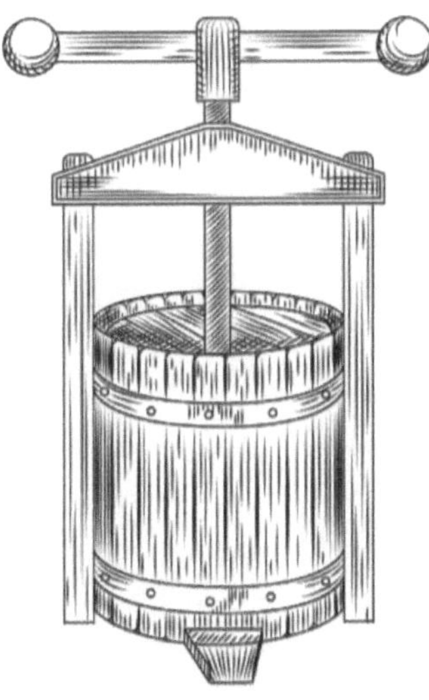

Andrew Lafleche

Copyright© 2020 Andrew Lafleche
ISBN: 978-93-90202-49-2

First Edition: 2020
Rs. 200/-

Cyberwit.net
HIG 45 Kaushambi Kunj, Kalindipuram
Allahabad - 211011 (U.P.) India
http://www.cyberwit.net
Tel: +(91) 9415091004 +(91) (532) 2552257
E-mail: info@cyberwit.net

No part of this book may be reproduced or transmitted in any form or by
any means, electronic, mechanical, photocopying, or otherwise, without
the express written consent of Andrew Lafleche.

Printed at Repro India Limited.

Books by
ANDREW LAFLECHE

Ashes

No Diplomacy

Shameless

A Pardonable Offence

One Hundred Little Victories

On Writing

Merica, Merica, on the Wall

After I Turn into Alcohol

Ride

Grateful acknowledgement is given to the following publications where some of these poems originally appeared: *The Prairie Journal, The Nashwaak Review, The Poet's Haven: Darker than Fiction, A Pardonable Offence, Poetry South, Ekstasis Editions: Voicing Suicide, Flumes, Montana Mouthful and Lucky Jefferson.*

Contents

ONE

Lt Me

lt me think
    lt me think
lt me think f wehve bin here
befor
    hmmm   hmmm
bin watchen my feet a wile
sumtimes forget my hands
lt me think
    lt me think
hmmm   hmmm   you
no   et rilly is
    et rilly is

In This Other Life

I just got rolled
by a Chinese Amish
with biker backing, took
my moving van: furniture,
memories, objects from
then ascribed with
sentimental clinging.
Lowered me into a ditch
at gunpoint—not even
a .45, some pistol—
started her up, and took
off, horse and buggy trailing
carefree like: no big deal.
Leaving a torrent of tears
screaming, "life doesn't
understand the years"
until I drowned, in
this other life.

When You Come Home

They was handing out tickets
    for a trip across the pond;
New wardrobe, pack your bags for you,
    teach you the Way of the Gun—
Play a couple war games on the twice-way range—
Be a parade waiting for you when you come home—
    When you come home.

Before We Shipped Out

Before we shipped out there were these cream-coloured
cue-cards we had to complete—the kind you wrote
your speeches on in grade school—little things, pre-printed
with our blood type, eye colour, prominent scars/birthmarks
/tattoos, height, approximate weight (we'd lose some
in the desert—some, all), a small checkbox to indicate the
accuracy of the above, and a black underlined space, where
we were to write a code-word, something easy to remember
we could to tell the rescue team who busted into wherever
we were being held captive if during a firefight we were
captured and taken prisoner, they would know for certain
it was the right soldier they were bringing home.
I wrote carrots, I think, because I like carrots fresh from the
garden. It could have been potatoes, I wrote, because, well
I like them, too. Each day I head out to the shop, I see
the prisoner of war flag hanging on the wall, big letters, *You
are not forgotten*. But if I'm being honest, most days, I do.

On Days Like Today

On days like today, I'm certain I died over there;
Most days. Probing for some semblance of life
Approach the door of nobody home.

Ghost in a world obscured:
  The trees are trees, but they're not *trees*.
  And the phoebes sing, but is it a *song?*

What I see contrasted by everything else my
Eyes absorb.
All of it a projection
On the mounted canvas of existing—and I'm not sure,
Anymore.

That midsummer dream
My path splintering—one of me
Expired, blood feeding the sand—one of
Me here; but not here
With other splintered lives—or those yet to be.

Plagued contemplations fill my days, nary a soul
To stroke. I is not me, she said, pretending apathy.

It Wasn't the Mortality of Combat

It wasn't the mortality of combat
    which has afflicted me all these years;
It was my eagerness—no, my lust—to dispatch life,
    a blood offering to the desert eagles. Is my.
    A half-life I was certain would reach its
    elemental decline. And hasn't.
It wasn't the high-stress, extreme
    alert existence over there, returned
    to a normal life, here, proved so much
    difficulty reintegrating;
It was stripping down, or being stripped down
    to the essentials, coming home
    eyes critical to the lie of lives:
    the manufactured busyness, business
    hurrying to keep the system spinning
    less it tip over, keep it consuming itself;
    manufactured distractions, luminous
    screens designed to train the eyes blind
    like stepping inside from a cerulean
    sunshine sky—all a parrot reciting
    company lines, scripted and uploaded *en
    masse*—won't even turn the damn things
    off when they go to bed—makes a
    man dizzy, less you're spinning at the
    same speed—there are such things as
    sticks in spokes anymore, walls and;
I don't know. It's like my soul
    is two lobes: One groaning, pop smoke,
    cut ties, journey that lonely road into

the woods at night—hope in the morn'
to find myself inside Thoreau's camp
and not that of the UniB-or-Oklahomi
guy's; The other a hope that maybe
there is a pilot and she'll pull us out
of this tailspin—but mostly I think that's
just in the movies, L.A., or—
I don't know. Only that ten years ago,
this day, I boarded a tiny Ryan airplane
and it flew me someplace;
and now everything is different
and now everything is the same
and maybe. Maybe
one day, I'll get to leave this place,
but I don't believe that, really.

She Was Escaped, Somehow

witness to that cabby
getting plugged

watching the metre
climb behind the stoplight

drab black sleeve
black leather gloves

arm shoved through
the open window
passenger side

squeezed
his outstretched
finger
twice—

she didn't hear the second
one, fell to the running board
gripping her ears
crawled out the side
door, around back

wiped her finger
prints off the licence plate

she doesn't remember why

kept her head down
ran, mostly

and now she's hiding
out in this aura-lit
one bedroom, sheets hung
over the windows

door bolted, twice
hugging her knees
rocking in the corner
of the corduroy couch

t.v. low CNN company
smoking cigarettes
after other cigarettes

calling now and again
after midnight
whispering before
a dead tone:

she is me.

The Wall

a crypt
ghostly shadow
reminders
memories framed
pictures
beautiful dead to be
missing
in space and mind.

one day, I will
not wake up
lost to everything
everybody
become
spectre
where a portrait
once hung.

Leviathan Sits Above the Box's Lip

a box of unread books
stacked haphazardly as if one day
I'll get around to reading them

a long day's journey into the night,
fiddlehead, the variety of religious
experience, something by Huxley

I saw a shooting star tonight–seconds
after peering into the nocturnal sky–
streak and vanish, like a life spent

thirty-four years spun on this sphere
set piggy and the flies on the shelf
she asked–would you die for me?

With the Vine or Grapes Thereof

she had a freckle
same colour as her iris
anchored in the white
of her eye   im certain
close as we were

that morning   skinned
by the river   tangled in legs
and arms   strands of hair
braided in the stainless ballchain
catacomb hung from my neck

zealous to find meaning
as only the desperate
can muster zeal for meaning
where there is   none

Eleven Wooden Stairs

fatigued with countless weightings
up and down   and up   and down

stonewalled cellar lined in aged offerings
stoke the fire   morning and night

morning and night   mourning   and
exhausted staying course   holding fast

eleven wooden stairs keep us apart
divide us   here   on any given night

Shell of a Home Dusted

where the broom couldnt reach   or
where we didnt sweep behind
the space the refrigerator once stood

involute receipts faded on the counter
serve remnants of promises left behind

cupboards ajar   same as closet doors
hallways framed in shadows
where yesterday memories hung

Harking

that night we were laying in bed, my
head on your lap, your fingers running
through my hair, how you asked if I'd
washed behind my ears, seemed out of
place, but I thought back anyway, to
my last shower the day before, I hadn't
and told you so. you deflated, shifted
I sat up, said you wanted to catch me in
a lie. we must have turned on the t.v.,
all I remember is the doubt which
spouted from your words.

that weekend in the Ozarks, the little
one-bedroom log house with the loft
looking out over the forest at the end
of the steep river washed road
deer in the tall grass by day, Orion
shielding our nights. we made love
or something-like, I told you it hurt
each time I pushed, gentle as I could,
even. the rash. the raw. the accusations
joking at first, solemn in your silence.

the next morning you brought it up
said you found a forgotten tampon
soiled in rot, might account for my
abrasions, the smell—said you weren't
going to tell me at first; said it didn't
disprove anything, joking of course,

then silence—it was the difference
between you and me. it's where I first
realized for certain, on that long drive
back from the mountains, how you'd
make an end of what you can't undo.

Lilith

1.

we grow   and outgrow   and grow apart
   in the aperture of day
carried by winds we cannot see
   and those we cannot name
to survive as a memory   in souls beyond recall

2.

had i the heart to reach her where she lay
   as i held her when we first embraced then
heartless as i know her favour given
   would now she hold me close until the end

Pedestrian

waif and stray pursuit
    soma on usury
if not wise   bound   to learn

Piano Played in Minor Keys

laundry washed dried and dumped
on the unsheathed mattress
in the unused spare bedroom
set three days now.

dishes stained with grease
pots crusted with burnt pasta
or not quite burnt, still
embedded nonetheless
soaking stacked
for equally as long, longer
hard to tell, less that into the guest
plates now
and all the glasses have been used up
so only the coffee mugs
remain for filling water and wine; but
even those are counting
three in the back of the cupboard
above the microwave splattered
with too many uncovered meals and—

at least the empties are disposed of
first thing.
at least the crumpled packs of cigarettes
are thrown out each morning,
ashtray flushed, table wiped clean.
at least
there are those.

shades drawn even before the sun sets
doors locked, windows too;
protecting the world from, or
protecting from the world, or
something of both
depending on which scream
of memory sways.

yes, things are not going too well
at the moment; and yes, maybe
things won't ever be well again.

0≠1

i am too old to shoot up a school now
    and a quick jaunt down the trans-canada
threading strangers together is too soon
    forgotten; a walnut stock under chin
is bound to slip or so the prop'ganda
    threatens—besides, it reads same as woken
up froze in the snow, forty-below, nake'
    clutching the finest of empty gibson's.
this far gone over the narrow way must
    say: here lies what it's like to be a bat.

+

this kid had the same name as me, except
not the first or second letter, or
if he did, he neglected them; might have been
this disregard, the waste, or the gym coach
and civics teacher (who were the same person)
calling me the same as him, even
though on roll our names were clearly different.

more likely this kid, his loyalty was adrift.
private he was alright, thoughtful sometimes:
knew about model rockets and rom's and read
real books; could have made a best friend.
in the presence of the elite, however, he was
a dick—a poseur posturing where he didn't
belong with those who would never accept him.

he was an army reserve, which was bad-ass
which was cool: sneaking around the woods
with a rifle, getting paid to crush the obstacle
course after school; 'course he bragged about
this weekend warrioring—all the while bush
rolling up his sleeves for an iraqi game of
fisty-cuffs—step-daddy american, half-breed
canadian, appropriated apologetic patriotism
in the time of bowling for columbine
married to common teenage unpleasure—

+

gin blossoms over pine
sounds like a drink, or
the colour of a coffin—or,
you're such a fucking liar, alia.

+

he wore a weathered bomber jacket,
snug jeans faded, hugging pencil legs
hands wedged between thighs
hoodie cinched 'round a pallor face,
blue lips showing;
features like the deaded head
      lopping off a dredged body
on a silver screen mystic river—
putrid air near mortified,
motionless he lay adjacent
all the staring faces who hated him.

+

it was the kind of outfit
decorated with soviet gas masks
hung on faceless dummies
staked between mildew mottled cardboard bins
overflowing
with soiled trousers and matchless tunics
stained around holes which wouldn't align
inspected against the few noosed incandescents.

"see," he said. "the bullet has to get in there
tumble around some—make
a real mess near impossible to stitch up—then
it comes out different from when it came in.
it's what you call a clean kill." matter-of-fact
like the dummies snug in rubber green.

it was the kind of outfit
obedient to proverbs twenty-two
and six; sell even your younger brother
a butterfly knife or a pocket switch;
dark—but its own kind of bright.

+

in the chinkmart next door, a hallway hole
behind the cracked case head display

with tiny snap-shut baggies
a pinkie bigger than a thumbnail

painted with billiard eight-balls and x-mass
trees and little purple wizard caps—

a rolled up projector canvas would unroll
and be postered against a flashbulb

"wan-owe!" index reaching, "brish-cumbia!"
and a wave of the wrist like swatting a fly.

                    +

faces sullen
        clothing grey
                walking nowhere

walking fast
the people on the street
all look sad

                    but nobody
                cries
anymore.

                    +

"we get it zack—"
        "it's zac, actually."
"unless you have something to offer the class—"
        "an entire demographic of human beings—"
"we're discussing voter rights and the age of majority."
        "ga—"
"zack!"
        "it's zac. actually."

                    +

NotesFromtheUnderground
Che   BeyondGoodandEvil
BellJar AYoungContrarian
Catcher   IndustrialSociety
ThePrince CommunistMan
MeinKampf TheCookbook
APerfectDayforBananaFish.

+

he thought the lady on the bus had given him the evil eye, a
curse inflicted upon him and his wife; his children.
he was sure. his wife not so. at home they broke an egg
into a glass of water and understood that they had indeed
been cursed with the evil eye on the bus by the lady who sat'cross.
their supplications were answered: neither were possessed.

their three children, 4, 2, and 60 days were not so fortunate
god ordered them to die as demons cannot be permitted
to possess catholic children. the only chance for the children
to escape purgatory would be for their heads severed
the demons could then be cast and by god's will, the kids
their tiny souls would be rescued and taken home safely.

the wife instructed the husband to get the knives out the drawer
and to kill their children as the lord almighty had told.
the children started growling, and speaking like the husbands
mother, taunting, telling him he was not abram enough to do
what god had instructed. the wife tried to pin the 2-year-old
daughter against the plastic mattress, but she was too strong.

they poured water on her and she began shaking and spitting
the woman parent chose a knife, the husband started stabbing.

the girl screamed but would not die. the wife told the man parent to cut off her head. the child tried in vain to get away. the husband hacked at her throat until her head came free. neck blood spurted heavily as the body gave a last spasm and the screaming ceased.

the couple took the 2 month old, the 2 month old who was frothing and spitting speaking in a language they could not understand but was surely satan manifest. he stabbed at the babe, the wife held her in place and cried because she was only a baby and loved her more than anything. the husband told her not to cry about gods will. mother looked away as father, husband, struggled with the throat.

the once sharp knife was sharp no longer and would not slit skin. the wife gave him a new knife and with much strength, succeeded. the boy was saved for last because he had the most power. he ran from his parents. desperate ran because the demon did not want to leave the boy and knew that god was not forgiving to demons, and to hell he would return. the parents cornered him. the child bit.

the man, the husband, the father, he bled from the bite. the woman, the wife, the mother, choked the boy but his breath would not evaporate. indeed strongest of the three demons he was. husband stabbed. in a boys voice the boy begged his daddy to stop. the father knew the demon was only using the boys voice to trick him so he did not stop. he was the hardest for he was his only son.

with all three children all three demons destroyed, the parents, the husband the wife, they held each other and cried. they cried for their children. they cried for the grace of god in choosing them for such a sacrifice. they cried because they were going to jail and would not see each other again, so they cleaned. bagged each head. dragged each body to their own beds.

the crib for the babe. then they showered together to wash away
the blood. the husband suggested they make love one last time, and
she agreed. they made love and slept together in their own bed. in
the morning the police came and arrested the couple. they found
the bodies and heads of the children. their apartment had no
windows and was very small. the city condemned the building.

later it was bought to tear down and erect condominiums.

+

dress up busywork as business
    and walk around pretender—
forget the tawdry gem is but a stone,
    jewel—jewel box is what they buried
    the pharaohs in—jewel weed—
touch-me-not i'm so delicate
    i might fall to bits, less
    everything remain arranged
    precisely in such a way
    to need the other's existence—
mutual dependence, mutual
    assured destruction, wily
    roundabout way in this
    fleeing game—wily willy—
tricksters wily running the world round.

+

"oh—my—god. you should have seen him
    how pathetic it was. if he wasn't
    such a loser, i would have almost felt
    bad."

"i can't believe he thought you'd go out with
    him."
"i heard he lives in a tiny wratch-trap
    house."
"probably on welfare, i know he gets
    his clothes at zeller's. those shoes are def bi-
    way."
"he's never even made the volleyball
    team."
"none of the guys like him. even the re-
    jects."
"he's just so—"

                    +

take out every single one of those spoiled little rich kids. every jock. every fucking mean girl. line them up and execute them one at a time. feel the rush. people aren't naturally heroic so they'll just stand there crying as one gets picked off after the other. gun to forehead, "remember when you slapped my lunch tray out of my hands?" fuck you. bang. next. "remember when you pissed on my gym clothes when i was in the shower?" fuck you. bang. next. "remember when you said i had a bubble butt and that all the girls thought i was gross? you're going to be quite the looker yourself, half your brain painting the wall." fuck you. bang. bang. bang. bang. bang. get away with at least 60. three bullets for each, two in the chest one in the head, that's only 180 rounds. thirty in a magazine, six mags. you can carry at least double that so with one ar and 12 clips there's 120 kids. and everybody gets excited over 15? maybe those kids in colorado should have given their plan a little more foresight. what am saying, some-one has to pave the way, lay the foundation for us to build on. still, a little more forethought can go a long way. consider this: the class-room route, that's what, thirty kids in a concrete room, one exit? tag one and everybody panics. take the teacher first. she'll probably have her back to the class writing something dumb on the board. everybody freaks out and then spray the ones closest to you. a girl peaks her head out from under the desk, shoot her. somebody gets brave and yells at you, shoot him. go in there expecting to get everyone and do not leave until you do. pop. pop. pop. two in the chest, one in the head. this first class dispatched sets the rest of the school on high alert so now everybody is locked down; lights off, shades drawn, students under their desks. easy pickings. the police are standing by but they're not going come in the school without devising a plan, so there's time. already thirty kills under the belt so just move to the next class. no need to run. building on the shoulders of giants remember. kick in the door. shoot the lock. whatever. pop. pop. pop. another three magazines. another 30 kids. that's 60 kids and haven't even broke a sweat. see this is brainstorming, better idea already: why not wait for an assembly? get the whole school involved. chain the doors on the outside of the gym, come in through the only unlocked exit and unload. chaos. always is. just maintain distance and play tag all day. gonna cost more bullets but there's always a few pressure cooker kabooms could be prepared in advance. some pipe bombs in the old knapsack to be throwing. get creative. this is art class. go for the big numbers. 120. anywhere above 60 will start to impress. when the news reports 14 people died in an attack i'm like, 14 people? they must have been some stupid-ass punks. anything you can count on your fingers and toes is unremarkable by definition.

+

she stands
in the upstairs window
framed in stone
choker chain around her neck

stares across the water
over the rolling knoll
through the forest skyline

and steps with the setting sun

to become a shadow
in the disappearing past

+

the ring around the moon
a perfect circle
shadows cast lay atop
shadows already at rest.

stars seen in depth
sadden me, staring into a time
long passed; how to move forward
always looking back?

it hasn't always been this way
or maybe like stars
appearing eternal, burn bright
until one day they don't,
i will, too.

this moment admiring the moon,
contemplating after
the borrowed bottle of peach schnapps
battling melancholy and sadness
as daddy's shotgun lies on the table
shells strewn across the bench.

and then i wake
overtaken by stark blackness
open eyes, no light coming through.

chaos, my mind, end of its tether
voices, familiar ones
afar, muffled by the ringing in my ears.

consoling voices, assuring
voices, voices that parrot
"everything is going to be okay,"
but if everything was,
i wouldn't feel afraid like i do.

the ringing isn't a dinner bell
or alarm clock, but the droning hum
a gunshot echo inside four walls.

lying in darkness i question:
have i shot someone? have there been people here?
have i shot myself? is this what dying feels like?
why can't i see? why the ringing in my ears?

i can smell: burnt eggs.

i can feel: a hand pressed against my face
another supports my shoulder.

i recognize the sobbing voice
but hear it as a stranger's
and even if i could make it out
i don't want to.

questions continue:
could it be paramedics? a police officer?
am i in trouble? i am in trouble.
decide to stop trying.

this is trouble and if i am to live,
best to delay consequences
for as long as possible.

what is more embarrassing
than surviving a suicide?
or a homicide suicide?

i thought of the mess to be cleaned
by someone who'd rather not:
blood spray on the walls, on the mirror
pieces of grey matter stuck to the patio doors
overlooking the river.
the resale value will plummet.

why can't i remember?
who are these voices? why can't i see?
aware of thinking and recognition of
thinking thoughts.
existing on two planes i fight
to make sense of the question
above all questions: why?

letting go.
if this is suicide, years of torment
are moments away from nothingness.
if criminal offence, there is no escape.

i drift off, let go, mumble something
the ringing stops
my pain disappears with the voices

for the first time i exist in silence,
without torment, without noise,
floating on my back in the ocean
ears submerged.

if this be death,
welcome.

+

analysis paralysis in front
a thousand blue bins of threaded steel caps
for ends, shop rag wadding, magnesium
flints from flares, wiring in electrical
slate a.b.s. tubes, pungent yellow glue—
or; seasonal with propane, a hose, a
little tent and some red green tape, and—
     "whatchya building?"
a voice behind the orange apron asks, name
spelled in sharpie across the heart: arthur
"but everybody just calls me art.
seems you could go a couple ways, what you
got here—
     building or fixing to tear down?
reason is there's this clubhouse behind the
old armoury, meet there every thursday—
put rockets together, launch 'em after.
     always on the lookout for new members,
meeting tomorrow you wanna come by.

just bring yourself.
here, let me put this stuff back for you."

+

tomorrow, then. maybe tomorrow. yes.
always tomorrow.

Taciturn of Sorrow

be it
omission
commission
of fear
pride
mortify my flesh
impeach
me too
I am responsible
guilty
Peter before dawn
betrayer
of Christ
brother
mother and father,

                    all.

hunkered on
veteran laurels

          misfortunate in
          underestimation

addict's denial
peccant world
mark three and twenty-five.

awoke
sweated:
it is not too late
Kaizen's whys
applied

we can brake
before the crash
pullover
slow, at least
consult the map
before
not
becomes
is
too late,
                    beg.

TWO

From Your House

from your house   right now   you cant see me
strange as this may sound to a casual observer
                                        but you cant
how some nights you call on the telephone to say
from down in the valley looking up on the mountain
you can see a faint blush of the otherwise blackened
silhouette through the trees   which burns in my
bedroom window   and you knew i was home
well darling   tonight you wont   there is a cloud
descended and shes smothered everything   even
the smoke from the chimney sinks toward the ground
the birds   too   dont know what to make of it
                        i just thought i should let you know

The Return

Oh portent sky of deathless
life, consumer of all beings—

We were happy once, weren't we?

That first time daring our
toes in the frigid, early summer
Atlantic—eight hours we drove
no matter, through the
green mountains of the National
Forest, behind us then, now.

Ocean, over head and ears in,
'ventilating greedily
at the shore, children screaming
the way children ecstasy-scream
in unreined wonderment—the grey
above and below, overlooked
or imagined silver and gold,
cold—told by the blue of our lips
we played until we couldn't
control the shivers and Mamma
thought, "Maybe, we'd had enough
for one day," but promised
by and by, we'd return.

#

Desert deserted saw-toothed Ghar
reaching skyward like a clenched fist
knuckle peaks railing against—railing.

There is no water here,
anymore at least, less seated
in the Watchtower
palm loosely guiding the wooden
machine-gun stock, left and right
over the farmer field arcs.
Solar fire blazing high in the
eight bell sky, index eager
stayed by the trigger guard—thirsty.

Scorched directly
the sand melted in the glare,
shimmered beneath
the rebellious mountains—liquefied so,
if you closed your eyes and breathed
a breath deep, you could
smell the land before time, buried
under leagues of life-filled sea
opening your eyes to the scintillation,
yellow become cradling green
and in that moment we'd returned.

But this, this emerald calm
fool me once the maxim goes
better just to breathe
ahead the conspiring blow.

#

The Yucatan was the Promised Land
México: breezy, simple.
Stars and sand like Afghanistan
                without the blood.

Atlantic: grey, crisp—welcoming
this near the prime meridian,
still, the immature horizon's
bare seamount flaunted its lack.

Oh portent sky of deathless
life, consumer of all beings—

We'll be happy again, won't we?
And she replied, "Go west."

Baja, the Sea of Cortez
an emerald coastline
deepening toward the Pacific
sailing in the breeze
guarded by the mountainous range—
extended toward the clouded heavens
in offering—oh portent sky
of—of—protector of all beings;
long I've reckoned this day
my exile ends and I return home.

This Side of War

rill basin hill
snow fleeing angry sun
always now, then.

conifer boundary
last journey into the night
harvest moon crowning

woke this side of war
Phoebe sounding winter's end
no more bodies; bombs.

Beside Grandma's Rocker

a silver fox emerged from the woods at dawn   this morning
alertly navigating the sleeping   snowthawed   farmscape
oblivious my second storey vantage where i perch   behind the
window overlooking the garden   having drawn the curtains
to allow the early glow to accent this bedfurnished room i keep
unslept in   clean sheets and cases folded snug in the nightstand
pillows tucked in the dresser beside grandmas rocker   only
the tip of the runner can i see from my room   across the hall
where i retire after a day tending the garden   wandering the
woods   harvesting trees for next winter   kneel and pray
of habit mostly   earnest of late   crawl under the covers
stare up through the window whose curtains are always drawn
so if the sky permits a cloudless night i can fall into a sleep
as if it were my last counting the stars

                                        a silver fox emerged from the
woods at dawn this morning   ahead the sun igniting the tops
of the black spruce   and i thought of you

The Declivity of Scars – A Score

A mar, surface deep reveals the most startling tragedies
indefinitely large, returned by weeping for a stranger.
Skin akin to palisades behind a yawning cliff, escarpment
of injuries, damaged by wear; moral and emotive, borne
carried in memory, the declivity—if only all scars were.

Blue Jay tearing greedily at the shrivelled apple clung
to last years harvest, pecks desperately at the tree's limb
until the red sustenance falls free to the snow dusted
earth—stems marked and scored by the harvested fruit
bare now, under grey March sky, ready to blossom anew.

Wounded tissue healed, a scar wove in its wake, a score—
the starting point of choreographic number. Here lay
a notation, an account of life, the evidence of have
traversed piercing mortal threats in this disinterested world
an indebtedness to the miracle of continued existence.

The songwriter's adoration, glorification, there is a crack
in everything, for how else would the light get in?
Skin akin to musical compose, stark, inescapable reality
braille under the brush of a loved one, shared; beholden
to scores by a life which doesn't understand the years.

Of Love

Blue ice drawn with ravenous slate eyes
        wide in serendipity—
pregnant verdure on the leeward shore
        swollen under the brush of withheld rain
surfeit openings by a lovers estrous embrace.

The earth sighs, a chortling brook
        spilling its abundance in lamblike gaiety
        as solstitial warblers climb the mountain
        offering incense to the cloistered puritan air.

Spring's kiss: a saccharine tonic
        chilled on a tentative tongue,
mistress of winter, mother, of replete adoration—
        how luscious is your savouring.

Spring at Wander Hill

Needles—
green confused with grey-greens, lift with the sharpening dawn.

The last constellations stand guard in the western eggplant sky:
Pyxis, Vela, Centaurus, assuring order at the boundary of night.

The marsh, a bin of cattails, captures the early light, suspends it
like a web 'cross paperback trees, ephemeral as an overdrawn
thought—obscuring reflections.

Yellow anemones sprung from the stone foundation of a tiny,
stove-heated home, accent its windows, shutters peeled back
to reveal the octothorpe muntins reddening beneath

                              the first colour of sun.

Two phoebe's, arranged in tandem on the clothesline—flit off
and return in some peristeronic choreography, sing: *fee bee fee
bee, wit-wit-wit.*

Even the piffling birds—the purple finch, the field and house
sparrows, others—are busy among the slanted grass bootlegging
linseed. Weed seed; a hint of vinegar livening the air.

The lilies and rhubarb muscle through the frozen earth—frozen
no more—bestial or stoic in their rise, far too early to tell.

Only sparse evidence of winter's carapace remain:

A single patch of snow on the hillock making a hasty retreat into
the dark woods to escape as a rivulet down the north face slope;

The dead leaves have yet to be reborn on the limping branches
from which they were brushed;

And, the deer are not here—nor have the black bear and her cub
emerged from their lethargy; but they will.

The dissonant timber in the woodshed are sounding so.

Identic

a fiddlehead sprung
in the first step of a fawn
this right side of april
scarcely adjacent the city
where the husbandry of more
comfortable   illusions
find difficulty laying root

logy clouds ease the glare
a moment   releasing
shadowbound vees in lies led

something not quite saccharine
tinting the air   a stilled voice
kicked up from
      i dont know where
maybe shes always been calling

a pair of mallards circle
      an infants mobile
honking   mouthing silence
even they   are eager
to become repetitions

Thankful or Afraid of Losing

aged wood returned to ash
by dawns new flame
sixty roasted coffee beans   hand selected
ground into the perfect press
the uncluttered   sunlit desk placed east toward
the blooming orchard
the forest entrance
the eagles nest overlooking the meadow
where the spring fawns lay nestled intimate
their mothers   beyond eye reach
glowing in gratitude or yellow in fear
of all done taken away   again

Okay Starless Night

you win.
here's my towel.
just leave the pillow
I fall asleep to each
night;
clinging
to, in a bed
one size too large.
leave me that
at least.
she did.
you're not worse
than her, are you?

The Northern Flicker

there he was   griege headdress full stopped
by a mars flame of nape   direct eyes
enshrined in cinnamon   the contrast
all possible tragedy   high stature of calm
beneath each   a stark indigenous mar drawn
across the carotid   piercing dagger bill
proud armadillo carapace over shoulders
onyx halfmoon necklace adorning chest
an innocence dress   sequenced with sable
hemmed goldenrod   reserved   of course
for flight   in the meadow   digging for ants

I've Took to Burning Books I'll Read No More

I've took to burning books I'll read no more,
even my own tossed to flame become smoke;
though less of those and most what people gift.
You should see some of the fires we have here,
away from that civil society,
where we can pepper the side of the hill
with bird shot and NATO rounds from the war—
borrowed of course, but nobody complains—
like our stories and wine and all who age
refined by every year enriched with time.
A page from the daily, some brush—a light,
we'll have this sucker scorching directly.
Bring a book, something you won't check again.
We'll shoot the guns, drink whisky, get lost some.

Broken Mirrors on Thundercloud Skies

The first one impressed:
tips of wings outstretched

spider legs clambering from the mist
sable silhouette soaring.

And then another, twice more,
palpable malevolence.

There is something in the air, here
you can see it in their eyes.

Fog risen birds of ill omen, broken
mirrors on thundercloud skies.

For Why Did I Come?

was it for the raven oil stain on the single
patch of chlorotic grass among the lingering white
he who squawks his taunt neverlearn neverlearn
never learn n e v e r learn neverlearn until i
look up and him with a choreographed precision
which in knowing shames worse than the provocation
takes flight silent now less for his herculean
wings compressing the air beneath is that why
to watch the bastard climb into the grey

Little Stone House

little stone house   in the forest
single room   wood stove   who
built you   scraped the earth
by which you stand   carried the
rocks dug from   set them carefully
in place   framed both windows
the thresholds   stovepipe   secured
the roof to keep out the rain   who
believed this trifling labour enough
show me the man who worked years
without praise   i wish to thank him
least lay my eyes upon   who he had
to become   to birth this monument
and leave it behind   an offering

All Souls Night

i.

potato gravy and mutton
late october eve
sweater snug
wool worn
reading under candlelight

blanket draped over lap
slippers slipped
tea steeped steaming
beside the recliner
needle at records end

out of reach

ii.

wine glass windowpanes
spider the rain

set upon grey skies
and greyer trees

pine needles weighted
shiver fall and rise

persuasive breeze threatens gusts
determined jays peck greedily

the feeder wavers
as if it will rain forever

iii.

leave trees falling to the sky
raindrops erupting through
the grass green canopy overhead
harbingers of darknesss children
raise their eyes
seekers of light peer below

iv.

birth   death   and memory
in the stargazers april bed
as robins search the snow dusted
slumbering grass encasement
for green shoots rising from
the hollowed stalks of a year past

v.

the white sands of dead decembers
stayed only by a spring
      which glimpsed its own death
in the breeze of a droughtborne summer
whose chaff would deny all harvests plenty
ahead the high fog's return
      to smother the terrene again

An Honest Prayer

and sanguinary by first light
waiting for the fog to lift to
diffuse these lurking spirits
into nothingness

oh   forgotten griefs
                is there one
who could name each of you

notes longing to rest
on absent ears
minor they be
risen from harmonious keys
anymore
will the music be regarded

suffice over the wreckage

On This Sunday Morning

overtop the trembling
aspen
raindrops fall
before striking the pain

Winds

wail louder　　winds
i hadnt want to be outside today
anyway
　　deride with all
your might　　i am well　　i
have a book　　i have a fire　　i have my pen

When the Pain Leaves

the well is covered   only the peak of the truss
visible   half way up the barn too   catacombed
poppies   fresh tracks perimetering the house
across the knoll   through the garden   circled
back unto the woods   negative twenty
furnace pumping heat in long gestations   lights
burning this near february eve   in the spring
it will be different   green   not   subzero
all this melted away   when the pain leaves

Healing the Orchard

growing down is growing the wrong way
　　　across the plane cant bear the weight
straight up wont produce any fruit
　　　a branch turned in on itself goes too
　　　the great teachers parable and all that
and be sure to let alone a few shoots
　　　　　　theyre next years apples
but dont worry　　these trees are forgiving
　　theyve been around here a while

Snow Forsaken by the Moon

reveals the grey of afterday   blown
by the easterlies   settled aloft the waning
overbalanced barn of yesteryear

regard the martens tiny snowshoe prints
along the shadowed knoll   stalking
the scent of a fresh kill   abandoned
beyond the umbrage   thicker than night

buried beneath the banks she treads
are all the wraiths   hauntees and hauntors
longing for spring   yearning
to be born again   someplace renewed

*

embers erasing back hand hairs with each bavin bestowal
coals breathing evanescent silvers   infernal reds   glints
of heaven wholly in being

nine days shy of gregorians april   modicum crystals   flecks
bellow across the knoll in valedictory farewell
                                    or so one might hope
the black and white warblers of yesteryear have returned and skirt
from branch to perch in their weesee weal   stood off
from the jays tearing greedily at the wearily hung shrivelled
remains of the tree of good and evil

judicious sun   supplicant receiver   deposed above and below
however lowseason the druthers dreary
one path ascends beyond the vista   the other edges   into the
eclipse

*

what resistance remains
screams   seared   steam   snuffed
by the gage pledged   it is too late
robins clash in brick terracotta flourishes
phoebes drum time from safe on their shelves
the youngest trees   shivering but yesterday
too thomas to have shed their inaugural frond
stand now   assured by their towering
elders   those keeping joined earth and sky
nodding condonation   it is time
thunderheads marching advance the cavalry
a thousand horsemen upon the morning fog
hear   hear   hearkening   hosanna
kneel   for spring has arrived

From Self to Self This Offering

Myself to myself.

1.

Remembering that I must die realizing I have yet lived—horror!

If were be today, what said-if at all-scrawled on the marble
marking where my body lay, until, at last, it too decays—returns?

Stare at this blackened stone of mind, mine eyes cannot discern
a trace of words, word, set to sum these thirty-four years of
waste.

Disgusted disposition; flag limply hung.

2.

The sun will have none of this late fallen white
anger rising against aquamarine sky
clouds all but vanished—stragglers scrambling over the summit.

The rhubarb bleeds through the ebony earth, as it must.

3.

Desk washed in scribbled pages
words of those come gone left
journals exacting judgment
evidence mounted all the years

abreast—ten let the record show!
Same,
　　same
　　　　same sea of sin evil.

Dismissed enigmatic laid bare by my own pen

　　　　　　　　Year
　　after year,
year.
　　　　　　　　　Year.

　　5.

Aged pine set on delirious coals
fevered by the proffer—the spider
too late in its rest rushes escape
pantomatic as checked
　　quits to the insatiable flame.

The condemnation of the Damascus Jew echoed in the whirring
　　dungchen wail: the wine press is prepared.
　　It is wanting.
　　It will be fed.

Come, have a drink, won't you?
　　Bottles drained down pipes flowed to springs feeding the
　　herbage these bare feet set upon.

Miasmic baptism dripping:
　　I stepped into the forest's twilight and wander alone.

8.

Yellow-bellied sapsucker clinging to the barn,
phoebe on the highest shoot keeping safe from
harm.

The night I decided if I could kill Christ I would, I cried,
    "Present me my accuser!"

13.

Saltwater deadman submerged ears drowning
      sinking into a night afloat below.
Young cunts salivate
      over soldiers eager for   blood.
Clip the razor to the page,keep it close.

Tell me something I don't already know
      of the nested chickees screaming
      as the marten claws the branch.

I plant your tree beside my pillow and dream it roots each night:
      sometimes the birds devour you;
      sometimes there are rocks—you spring and wither;
      sometimes thorns;
      sometimes ants;
      sometimes buds—my favourite of dreams
      dared over
      dawn becomes you.

21.

Damn the browned maple leaf
Shrivelled and tumbling with the winter breeze
Ass over tea kettle, uphill, across the snow.

Damn the opaque icicles dripping
In the warmer single degree, clouded at root
Their crystal apexes' distorting the view
—Refracting iridescence, casting flood promises.

Damn the lone snow bunting hesitative on
The feeder, its black beak, wings and tail.

Damn the lumbering pine boughs
The rotted oak snapped in two, the tangled
Apple branches still clinging to harvest's fruit.

Oh, painted window of stubborn glass,
Permit this fist against your pane!

How thou mock me, this wretched morn,
Death to the sun, Evermore! Again.

34.

I know Death in the snap of the bullet I didn't perceive.

I know Death in my fingers looking forward to the kill.

I know Death in the last secreted breathe of the infant in my lap.

And I know Death's uttermost woe in a daughter's wail kidnapped at gunpoint, "Daddy!"

And I to Death give my back, these eyes bleed to know no more.

55.

Fragments of memory, minutia of usage expired
without past, tomorrow leagues deeper than the sea,
wider than the eye of the needle,
indefinitely.

Integral—any dharma whose derivative is a given dharma,
Function—the moment my life had worked me for as all the world dies.

89.

From self to self this offering, myself to myself.

Eyes Wide

toronto i have seen you   montreal
kebec   saint john   st johns and charlottetown
with her of halifax   saskatchewan
winnipeg   victoria   vancouver
regina   edmonton   that wretched mall
calgary   olympic park   ottawa
i have seen you all   your women   your streets
your bars and offices and acclaim and
i   canadian   am shamed   i have seen
nothing   all of these sojourned days

www.ingramcontent.com/pod-product-compliance
Lightning Source LLC
Chambersburg PA
CBHW031000180726
47993CB00018B/1199